WISDOM
of
OWLS

A FIREFLY BOOK

Published by Firefly Books Ltd. 2024
Copyright © 2024 Moseley Road Inc.

First printing

Library of Congress Control Number: 2023949122

Library and Archives Canada Cataloguing in Publication

Title: Wisdom of owls / compiled by Lisa Purcell.
Names: Purcell, Lisa (Editor), compiler.
Identifiers: Canadiana 20230572863 | ISBN 9780228105107 (hardcover)
Subjects: LCSH: Quotations, English. | LCSH: Wisdom—Quotations,
   maxims, etc. | LCGFT: Quotations.
Classification: LCC PN6081 .P86 2024 | DDC 080—dc23

Published in the United States by
Firefly Books (U.S.) Inc.
P.O. Box 1338, Ellicott Station
Buffalo, New York 14205

Published in Canada by
Firefly Books Ltd.
50 Staples Avenue, Unit 1
Richmond Hill, Ontario L4B 0A7

Moseley Road Inc.
International Rights and Packaging
22 Knollwood Avenue
Elmsford, NY 10523
www.moseleyroad.com

Printed in China | E

WISDOM
of
OWLS

Compiled by
Lisa Purcell

FIREFLY BOOKS

"When the *owl sings,* the *night* is *silent.*"

~ CHARLES DE LEUSSE

"The *inauspiciousness* of ***the owl*** is ***nothing*** but the *inauspiciousness* of ***the man*** who ***thinks*** that owl is *inauspicious!*"

~ Mehmet Murat ildan

*"**Towering** genius disdains a **beaten path. It** seeks regions hitherto **unexplored.**"*

~ Abraham Lincoln

"Though *what* bird in the *best* of circumstances does *not* look a *little* stricken?"

~ LORRIE MOORE

"*Hope* is the
thing with feathers
that *perches in the soul*
and *sings the tune*
without the words
and *never stops at all.*"

~ EMILY DICKINSON

"Be **who** you *are* and *say* **what** you *feel,* because those who **mind** *don't matter,* and those who **matter** *don't mind."*

~ Bernard M. Baruch

"**Well**, in this *world* of *basic stereotyping,* give a guy a **big nose** and some **weird hair** and he is *capable* of **anything.**"

~ Frank Zappa

"**Some** *people* would regard *people* who *look* *like* **they** *do* as *ugly* **if** they *did* **not** *look like* **them.**"

~ Mokokoma Mokhonoana

"*He looked* at *me* as if *I* was a *side dish* he *hadn't ordered.*"

~ RING LARDNER

"*We* have *always*

held to the *hope,*

the *belief,*

the *conviction* that there

is a *better life,* a *better world,*

beyond the

horizon."

– FRANKLIN D. ROOSEVELT

"If there's **one thing** I'm *well versed in* it's *my* **own** *good qualities.*"

~ Patrick Rothfuss

"She *tried* to smile *sympathetically*, *but* with her face it wasn't *quite* possible."

~ Anthony Horowitz

"*Deal* with the *faults* of **others** as **gently** as *your own.*"

~ Chinese Proverb

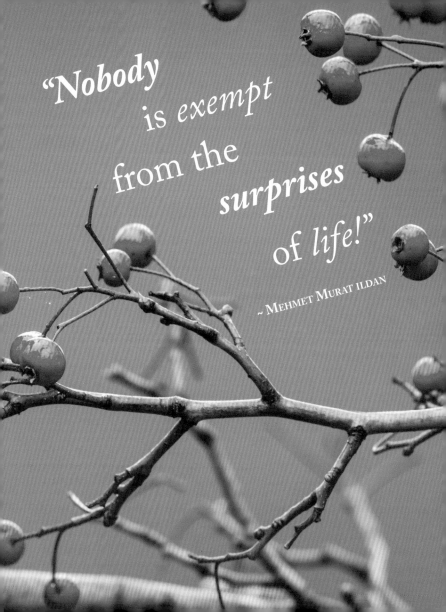

"Nobody is *exempt* from the **surprises** of *life!*"

~ MEHMET MURAT ILDAN

"A *skeptic* is ***one who knows too much*** for a ***fool,*** and *too little* for a *wise man.*"

~ H. W. SHAW

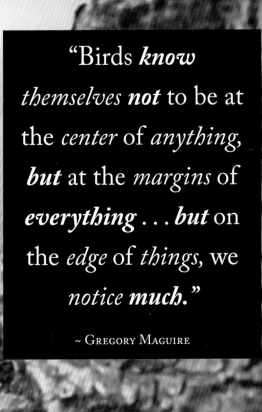

"Birds *know themselves* **not** to be at the *center* of *anything,* **but** at the *margins* of **everything** . . . **but** on the *edge* of *things,* we *notice* **much.**"

~ Gregory Maguire

"I *never* found a companion that was *so companionable* as *solitude*."

~ HENRY DAVID THOREAU

"At home,
I *love* reaching
out into that
absolute silence,
when you can
hear the owl
or ***the wind.***"

~ Amanda Harlech

"Then *nightly sings* the *staring owl,* **Tu-whit;** **Tu-who,** a *merry note.*"

~ WILLIAM SHAKESPEARE

"*The eyes are the windows of the soul.*"

~ THOMAS PHAER

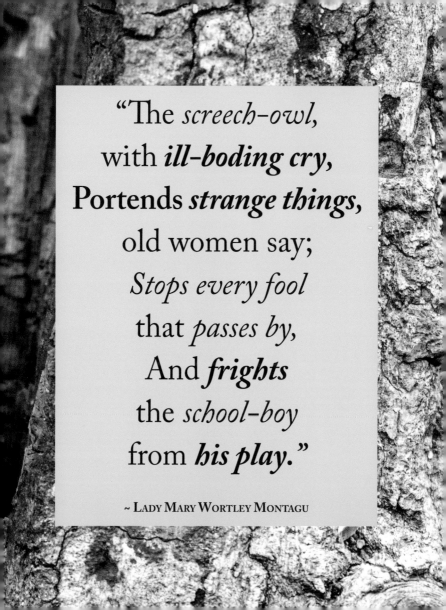

"The *screech–owl*, with ***ill-boding cry***, Portends ***strange things***, old women say; *Stops every fool* that *passes by*, And ***frights*** the *school–boy* from ***his play.***"

~ Lady Mary Wortley Montagu

"*Life* is a *journey,*
not a *destination.*"

~ CLIFF NICHOLS

"*Let* the
eye of vigilance
never be *closed.*"

~ THOMAS JEFFERSON

"A *fool* **thinks himself** to be *wise,* but a *wise man* **knows himself** to be a *fool.*"

~ WILLIAM SHAKESPEARE

"*O* you
virtuous owle,
The *wise Minerva's*
only fowle."

~ Sir Philip Sidney

"Success is *peace of mind*, which is a *direct result* of *self-satisfaction* in **knowing you did your best** to *become* the **best** you are **capable** of *becoming*."

~ JOHN WOODEN

"I'm *happy*.
Which often
looks like

crazy. "

~ DAVID HENRY HWANG

"*Perhaps* he **does not want** to *be* friends with *you until* he **knows** *what you* are *like.* With *owls* it is **never** *easy-come-easy-go.*"

~ T. H. WHITE

"A *proud man* is **always** *looking down* on *things* and *people;* and, **of course,** as long as you are *looking down,* **you cannot** *see something* that is *above you.*"

~ C. S. LEWIS

"The *clamorous owl,*
that *nightly hoots*
and *wonders*
At our
quaint spirits."

~ WILLIAM SHAKESPEARE

"No bird soars too high if he soars with his own wings."

~ WILLIAM BLAKE

"A *dream*
you ***dream alone***
is **only** a *dream.*
A *dream* you
dream together
is *reality.*"

~ JOHN LENNON

"*If* you're *always*

trying to be normal

you will *never know*

how *amazing*

you **can** *be.*"

~ Maya Angelou

"There was a *wise old owl* who *sat in a tree.* The *less he spoke* the *more he heard.* The *more he heard* the *less he spoke.* *Why* can't *we be like* that *wise old owl in the tree?*"

~ PAUL RICOEUR

"I'm **already** an excellent *flyer*. **Maybe** I can *fight crime* too."

~ EMLYN CHAND

"It is *not only fine feathers* that make *fine birds.*"

~ Aesop

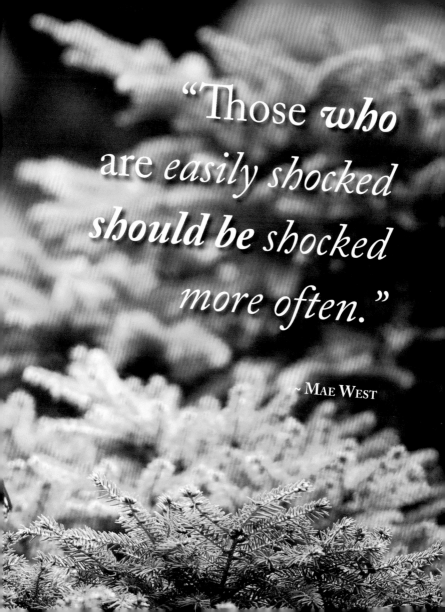

"Those *who* are *easily shocked* **should be** *shocked more often.*"

~ MAE WEST

"*If* you *surrendered* to the *air*, you ***could*** *ride it.*

~ TONI MORRISON

"It's **all in the eyes:** those *magnificent piercing optics* are what make **all owls** *look like* they are ***deep*** in *concentrated scrutiny* and *steeped in* **long-lost knowledge.**"

~ MATT SEWELL

"To *be* an *artist* means ***never** to* ***avert*** one's *eyes*."

~ Akira Kurosawa

"*Alone* we can do **so little;** *together* we can do **so much.**"

~ HELEN KELLER

"I got **you** to look after **me**,

and *you* got *me* to look after *you,* and *that's* why."

~ JOHN STEINBECK

"*When* people *complain* of your *complexity*, they *fail* to *remember* that *they* *made* *fun* of your *simplicity.*"

~ MICHAEL BASSEY JOHNSON

"Faith is the bird

that feels the light

when the dawn is still dark."

~ RABINDRANATH TAGORE

"The *more seriously* we *work* on our *own imperfections,* the **less** we are *judgemental* of the *imperfections* of **others.**"

~ Neal A. Maxwell

"*Love* is a *springtime plant*
that *perfumes* **everything**
with its *hope* . . ."

~ GUSTAVE FLAUBERT

"*My friends call me* an *owl. Apparently,* it's a *combination* of *being wise* and *having big eyes.*"

~ ROMY MADLEY CROFT

"If you *can't fly*,

   then run,

if you *can't run,*

   then walk,

if you *can't walk,*

   then crawl,

but by *all means*

   keep moving."

~ MARTIN LUTHER KING JR.

"It is *better* to *be alone*

than in *bad company.*"

~ GEORGE WASHINGTON

"*St. Agnes' Eve*—
Ah, *bitter chill*
it was!
The owl,
for *all his feathers,*
was *a-cold.*"

~ JOHN KEATS

"An *owl* is
mostly air."

~ Ursula K. Le Guin

"The *little owls* call to *each other* with **tremulous, quavering voices** throughout the *livelong night,* as *they sit* in the *creaking trees.*"

~ THEODORE ROOSEVELT

"An **owl** is the *wisest* of **all birds** because the ***more*** *it sees* the ***less*** *it talks.*"

~ CHRISTIE WATSON

"We must accept finite disappointment, but never lose infinite hope."

~ MARTIN LUTHER KING JR.

"The **best** *way*
to make
children **good**
is to *make*
them **happy.**"

~ OSCAR WILDE

"The *owl* is one of the *most*
curious creatures.
A *bird* that *stays awake*
when the **rest**
of the *world sleeps.*
They can **see in the dark**.
. . . *What* does **he see** and
what does **he know** that
the *rest* of the *world*
is **missing?**"

~ M. J. Rose

"*Owls* are known as *lonely birds*; but it is not *known* that they have **the** *forest* as their **best** *friend!*"

~ MEHMET MURAT ILDAN

"*An owl* is **traditionally** a *symbol of wisdom,* so **we** are **neither** *doves* nor *hawks* **but owls,** and *we are vigilant* when *others are resting.*"

~ Urjit Patel

PICTURE CREDITS